Introduction

This book covers the north part of Perthshire – an area often referred to as Highland Perthshire. As this name suggests, it is a mountainous region where deep glens, with rivers and lochs, intersect the hills.

The area runs from Loch Tay in the south to Glen Garry in the north, and from Rannoch Station, west of Loch Rannoch, past Loch Tummel to Loch Faskally in the east. The land between the principal valleys is mountainous, mainly covered in heather moorland: the home of grouse, deer, mountain hares and golden eagles. In contrast, the flat ground in the broad straths is fertile farmland, whilst the lower hillsides are covered in rough grassland used for grazing sheep and cattle.

Many different types of walking are available in the area, from gentle riverside strolls (*5,16,17,22,24*) and short forest walks (*17,27*) to Munro bagging – climbing mountain peaks over 3,000 feet high (*7,11,26*). In between there are short but energetic circuits of waterfalls (*8,20,23,25*) and long, scenic routes along old drove roads through the hills (*1,2,3,4,10*). Because most of the terrain is far from flat, some of the shorter walks and many of the longer ones involve a fair amount of climbing.

Scattered throughout the valleys are attractive towns and villages where you will find accommodation, shops and other services. The largest centre is the Victorian town of Pitlochry, which developed as a holiday resort when the railway arrived in the mid-19th century. There are many interesting walks around the town. The Loch Faskally walk (*16*) crosses Pitlochry Dam, where you can watch salmon negotiate the fish ladder, whilst the Black Spout walk (*20*) goes via a splendid waterfall to one of Scotland's smallest distilleries at Edradour. The energetic will enjoy the views on the walk to Grandtully (*21*) and from the summit of the National Trust for Scotland's Craigower Hill (*19*). Hill walkers should not miss climbing Pitlochry's own mountain, Ben Vrackie (*15*) and then relaxing at the 300-year-old Moulin Hotel, which brews its own beer.

The Wade Bridge – Aberfeldy

The other main centre is Aberfeldy, which is situated where the Wade Bridge crosses the River Tay. General Wade, who, after appointment as Commander-in-Chief of the army in Scotland in 1724, built 28 bridges and 250 miles of military roads, had his headquarters at the Weem Hotel. This is adjacent to the Weem walk (*27*) and Castle Menzies, a particularly fine example of a Z-plan tower house, which has been restored by the Menzies Clan Society. In the unspoilt market town of Aberfeldy you can walk from the Square up the picturesque Birks of Aberfeldy (*23*), where the Moness Burn cascades over waterfalls in a tree-clad gorge above the town, or follow the River Tay to Grandtully (*22*).

Just down the road on the shore of Loch Tay lies the estate village of Kenmore, which was established by the lairds of the Campbell clan. On the Kenmore walk (*24*) you can see many of the buildings that the Campbells, who became the Earls of Breadalbane, erected – including the 400-year-old Kenmore Hotel and the gates for Taymouth Castle (completed 1842). Drummond Hill (*27*), which rises behind Kenmore, is notable as the place where Capercaillie (large turkey-like birds which inhabit conifer woodland) were successfully reintroduced to Scotland in 1837. At the nearby Falls of Acharn (*25*) there is a surprise viewpoint in a Hermit's cave and, on the opposite side of Loch Tay, you can walk up Ben Lawers (*26*), Scotland's tenth highest Munro.

The next major valley to the north of the Tay contains Loch Rannoch, Dunalastair Water and Loch Tummel. The focal point is the village of Kinloch Rannoch, with its attractive riverside and hill walks (*5,6*). The walks start from the Square, where there is a monument to Dugald Buchanan, a local scholar, evangelist and poet, who died in 1768. Nearby you can walk up the 'Fairy hill of the Caledonians', Schiehallion (*7*), or northwards from Loch Rannoch to Dalnaspidal (*4*) via Loch Garry.

Two of the longest and most remote walks begin 20 miles west of Kinloch Rannoch and cross the empty wilderness area of Rannoch Moor – the scene of David Balfour's escape from the redcoats in Robert Louis Stevenson's *Kidnapped*. They start at Rannoch Station (*1*) and Corrour (*2*), which is only accessible by train or on foot.

North by road and rail from Pitlochry is Blair Atholl, the estate village beside Blair Castle – seat of the Dukes of Atholl, who maintain Britain's only legitimate private army. From here you can climb hills (*11*) walk up beautiful glens on the Atholl Estate passing ruined shielings where peasant farmers used to live (*9,10*) or follow an old route through the hills to the west (*12*). The nearby Falls of Bruar (*8*) were visited by Scotland's national poet, Robert Burns, who wrote verses begging (successfully) the then Duke of Atholl to plant trees on their rugged sides.

Whichever walks you do, you'll find something of interest, from ancient standing stones (*21*) and Allean's ring fort (*27*) to the Soldier's Leap in the Pass of Killiecrankie (*14,16*). Enjoy your walking in this magnificent area in the heart of Scotland.

Castle Menzies – Weem

1 Rannoch Moor — A+

A linear walk along the north edge of a great natural wilderness. The firm tracks and boggy paths provide wide views of shimmering lochs and moorland encircled by mountains. **Length: 12 miles/19km** (one way); **Height Climbed: 600ft/180m** (east to west).

O.S. Sheets 41 & 42

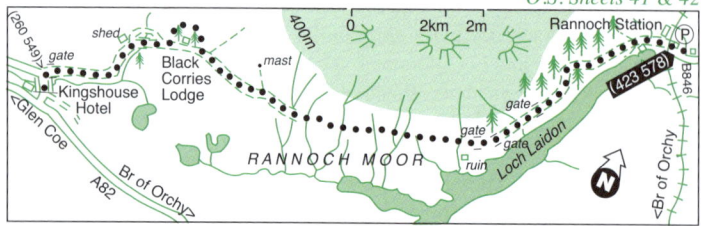

This walk can be done in either direction but the views are best walking west, from Rannoch Station to the Kingshouse Hotel. The route ends are a long way apart by road but it is possible to make a circuit using the bus from Kingshouse to Bridge of Orchy and the train to Rannoch Station. Alternatively you could walk both ways, possibly with an overnight stop (there are hotels at either end).

Start from the car park at the end of the B846 road to Rannoch Station. By a white cottage, take the signposted track which crosses the railway line then heads towards a conifer plantation.

When you reach the trees the track splits. Keep left, passing the two entrances to a white cottage by a lochan before reaching a junction at the end of Loch Laidon. Go right here, into the trees.

Follow this track for three miles/5km, through conifers (the views are very limited here, but open up later).

The track eventually ends at a metal gate and a turning bay. Beyond this there is a short stretch of boggy path before you finally leave the trees at a further gate and the full breadth of the moor becomes visible. The path beyond is rough and faint in places, but always runs close to a line of electricity poles crossing the moor.

After 2½ miles/4km you reach the start of a gravel vehicle track. Follow this, ignoring turns off to the right, to reach the edge of the trees around Black Corries Lodge. The footpath goes uphill, outside the fence, and returns to the track on the far side.

As you approach a second stand of trees, the track splits. Keep left, downhill, with fine views of Buachaille Etive Mór ahead.

Beyond the estate gate there is a junction. You have now joined the West Highland Way and can continue to walk in either direction (*see* 'Walks Fort William'). A turn to the left quickly leads to Kingshouse Hotel.

2 Corrour to Rannoch Station — A+

A linear walk on hill tracks over remote moorland surrounded by high mountains. Travel to the start by train then return on the 'Road to the Isles' past pretty Loch Ossian. Length: **11½ miles/18km** (one way); Height Climbed: **550ft/170m** (west to east).

O.S. Sheets 41 & 42

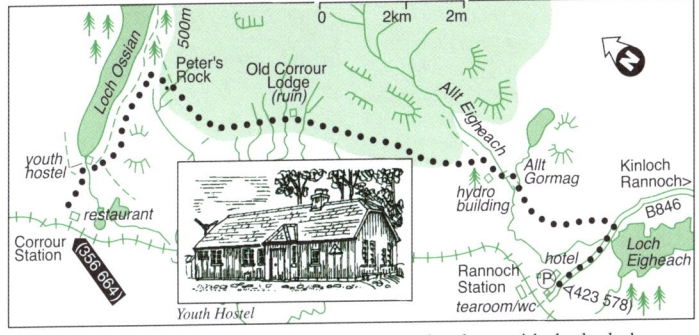
Youth Hostel

Reach Rannoch Station by following the B846 along the north side of Loch Rannoch and on past Loch Eigheach to the end of the road. Beyond lies vast and empty Rannoch Moor. Corrour, which cannot be reached by road, is the next stop on the railway to the north. Check the timetable in advance and allow plenty of time on the winding roads to reach the station.

Leave the train at Corrour and cross the line to the side with the lone building. Follow the track that leads eastwards towards Loch Ossian. At a junction of tracks go straight on towards the Youth Hostel on a wooded promontory, but as you approach it keep right at a fork. Level with the Youth Hostel, turn right onto a clear track.

After a short distance the track forks. Keep left, curving left to climb across the slope with the loch down to your left. Near the top of its climb, the track turns hard right, quickly passing Peter's Rock (which has a touching inscription) then continuing across the open moorland with fine views to the south. Two miles/3km beyond the rock the track passes the ruins of Old Corrour Lodge, with its pale grey granite walls.

3 miles/5km beyond the Lodge, the track passes a plantation and bends right, passing a small Hydro building before crossing Allt Eigheach on a vehicle bridge. Beyond this, it continues by the river for a short distance, crossing Allt Gormag on another bridge, before edging left, away from the river.

After 2 miles/3km join the public road and turn right to walk 1½ miles/2.5km back to the start.

3 Carie to Innerwick _____ A

A linear walk along an old drove road between Loch Rannoch and Glen Lyon; good tracks through conifer forest but rough on the moorland section. Can be done in either direction. Length: **7 miles/11.2km** (one way); *Height Climbed:* **1000ft/300m**.

O.S. Sheet 51

This walk follows the route of the old 'Kirk Road' which residents living by the side of Loch Rannoch used to take to get to the little church in Innerwick. To reach the start, follow the south Loch Rannoch road for 3 miles from Kinloch Rannoch to reach the Forestry & Land Scotland car park at Carie.

At the far end of the car park there is an interpretive panel. Take the path to the right of it (yellow/blue/red). After a short distance go right again (yellow/blue/red) to reach a 4-way junction. Turn left onto a track. Soon after, ignore a left turn by an old wall (blue/red) and carry straight on (yellow), climbing steadily, with the sound of the river eventually coming into earshot down to your left. Continue to a junction with a larger track (**A**). Turn left (signposted) and follow the track up to a gate at the forest edge.

Looking ahead, the rough track continues, climbing up the right-hand side of a wide valley to reach the watershed. Beyond this, the track crosses a stream on a plank bridge. Just beyond the bridge, ignore a track heading down to the right and continue on the main track, contouring across the hillside then descending.

As you drop, the track goes through a gate and enters a conifer wood. Ignore two tracks heading to the left

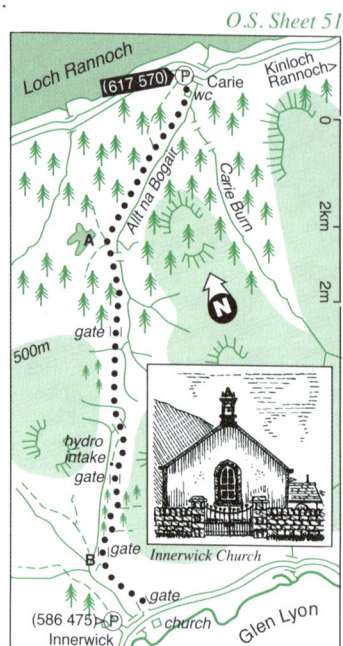

in the trees. Just beyond a gate at the bottom of the plantation you arrive at a junction (**B**). Stay on the main track to the left, which drops down through a woodland area to reach a gate leading on to the public road.

In trees on the far side of the road is the charming white church at Innerwick and there is a large car park and picnic area just beyond.

4 Loch Rannoch to Dalnaspidal _____ A

A linear walk following old hill tracks through a high pass and past remote Loch Garry. A steady climb then level walking on good tracks, apart from 1 mile/1.6km of wet moorland. **Length: 12 miles/19km** (one way); **Height Climbed: 950ft/290m**.

O.S. Sheet 42

Start at Annat, 2 miles west of Kinloch Rannoch on the B846. Here a track leaves the road for Annat Farm. Nearby a sign on the road indicates the path to Dalnaspidal. There is no room to park here.

Follow the track uphill for 300m to reach the farm, then go through two gates to the right of the buildings. A grassy lane climbs between trees and a stone wall. This leads to a gate on the right marked with a footpath sign. Pass through this gate and follow a track between two walls, turning hard left at one point.

At the top of this walled section there is a gate. An arrow points you up a rough track, which climbs to some old ruins. Keep right here, still on the track, fording a burn then climbing on towards a conifer plantation.

The track swings left on the near side of the plantation. When the trees end it continues over open ground to join another track coming up from the left (620 617). Keep right, then climb gently through a pass before descending to reach Duinish Bothy. Just before the cottage turn left for ½ mile/0.8km to reach a bridge over a river.

A track runs up the far side of the river. Cross this and bear half-right, aiming to walk at the foot of the steep slope to your left, but above the broken marshy ground to your right. In 1 mile/1.6km you will reach a gate at the end of the track by Loch Garry. This runs up the west side of the loch, passing a building where water is extracted into the Garry Tunnel to feed a hydro-electric scheme.

At the far end of the loch, follow the track across two bridges and on to a farm, then turn left over the railway line. (There is room to park just beyond.) Walk uphill to the A9, where the turning is signposted for Dalnaspidal.

5 **Kinloch Rannoch / 6 Craig Varr** _____ C/B

5) *A gentle stroll around Kinloch Rannoch along the river and hillside. Length:* **1-2½ miles/1.6-4km**; *Height Climbed:* **negligible**. **6)** *A short, steep climb to a fine viewpoint. Length:* **2½ miles/4km** *(there and back); Height Climbed:* **800ft/240m**.

O.S. Sheet 42

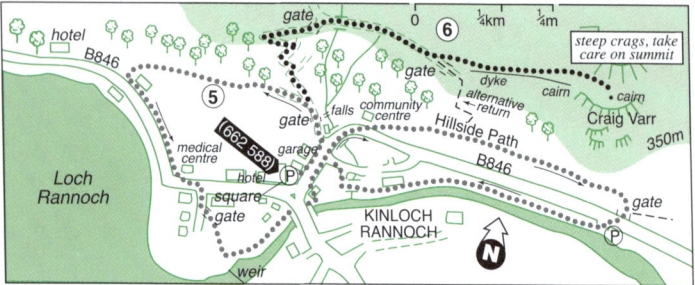

Park in the square in Kinloch Rannoch. Walk past the garage and go left up a signposted track beside a fine waterfall. Go through a gate to reach a junction. At this point you have a choice.

Walk 5) Head left on a path, passing behind a hydro-electric building, then running through open woodland to rejoin the public road just before the Loch Rannoch Hotel.

Turn left and follow a path – initially off the road then by the roadside. After a cottage go right through a gate ('Buchanan Path') and continue to a picnic area by a weir. Follow the clear path down river. Beyond the bridge climb left, back to the village square.

Pass the garage again and follow the main road to the Hub (Community Centre). Here, take the 'Hillside Path'. This runs above the road, staying right of a gate then crossing a footbridge. Beyond a gate it joins a broad track to contour below Craig Varr, then drops down to another track.

To return go right, through a gate, and cross the road. Follow the riverside path, through a parking area then on under trees. It becomes tarmac near the village and after a footbridge bends right to join a lane that joins the road opposite the garage.

Walk 6) Head right (signed 'Craig Varr') and follow the main, clear track as it climbs steeply uphill through birchwood, ignoring paths and tracks off to left and right. Continue to reach a gate at the edge of the trees. Go through this. When you reach a fork, go right (arrow), then cross a bridge.

Just before the next gate, leave the track and head left towards the line of a broken dyke. Follow this until a rough path heads left, away from the dyke, and climbs more steeply to the viewpoint.

Pause and admire the superb views before returning by the same route.

7 Schiehallion & Foss Loop _____ A+/C

A) *A steep climb up one of Perthshire's most famous Munros, mostly on good paths, but with large boulders near the summit. Length:* **6¼ miles/ 10km** (there and back)*; Height Climbed:* **2500ft/760m**. **B)** *A short woodland walk from the same car park, giving good views of the hill. Length:* **1 mile/1.5km**; *Height Climbed:* negligible. *O.S. Sheet 42 or 51*

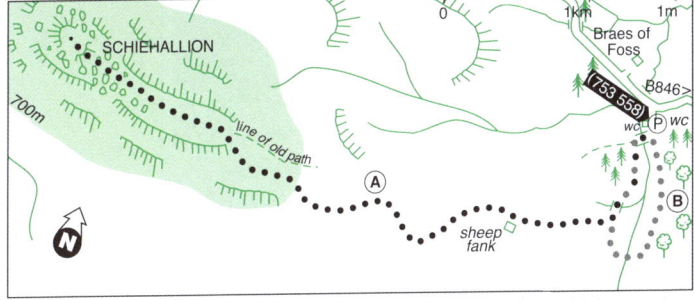

From the highest point of the B846 Tummel Bridge to Aberfeldy road a minor road cuts west signposted as 'Schiehallion Road'. Two miles along this road is Braes of Foss car park (fee): the starting point for these two walks.

Walk to the far end of the car park and start along a clear path. After a short distance the path splits. Here you have a choice.

For the short 'Foss Loop', keep left and follow the clear path through the trees of Dùn Coillich Community Woodland then back by the outward Schiehallion path.

To climb Schichallion, keep right. The clear path leaves the trees and sets off across open moorland to reach an old sheep fank. Beyond this the path begins to climb more steeply, and stone steps have been built at various points which ease the ascent. The route is never in doubt as the path winds up to meet an old path on a stony plateau. The views are superb.

On reaching the plateau head left (west) on a now faint path along the crest of the ridge. For over a mile/1.6km climb steadily up the ridge as the ground becomes more bouldery. As you approach the summit you have to scramble up bare slabs and over large blocks of rock balanced on top of one another. The top is usually windy, but you may find shelter behind a rock as you admire the distant views.

Return by the same route, taking care to stick to the ridge and not drift down to one side too early. The point where the path drops down from the plateau is very obvious.

8 Falls of Bruar _____ C

A steep rocky path clings to the edge of a deep, wooded gorge near Blair Atholl. This walk makes a circuit of the gorge using two bridges which provide stunning views of the waterfalls. Length: **1½ miles/2.4km**; *Height Climbed:* **350ft/110m**. *NB: path eroded in places.*

O.S. Sheet 43

The paths around the Falls of Bruar were laid out 200 years ago by the then Duke of Atholl. They are still a popular attraction. **Children and dogs should be kept under control as the paths run above cliffs.**

Start from Bruar, just off the A9 north of Blair Atholl. Park at the House of Bruar, a large visitor attraction with shops and cafés.

From the entrance to the car parks off the B8079, walk a few paces along the road in the direction of Blair Atholl to find a sign for the start of the walk. Walk left up the river bank; passing a cottage then under a railway arch, beyond which there is an information board.

A pleasant stroll through open forest leads to a rocky outcrop with a protective railing from where you can see the lower bridge. Below it there is a waterfall with a natural rock arch.

Descend the outcrop by wooden steps and continue up the rocky path until it forks. Go right and peek through the arch of the old viewing house. Then walk across the bridge, pausing to look down on the falls and gaze upstream into a deep pool.

Follow the well-worn path up the far side over bare rock and tree roots and continue to reach a bench positioned perfectly for viewing the

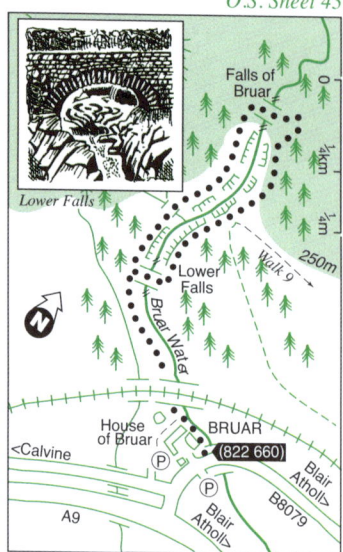

upper falls.

Continue uphill through the trees, on a path that eventually levels out high above the gorge. Carry on to a picnic area then bend left down to the upper bridge.

Enjoy the high vantage point of the bridge then go left on the far side on a path through darker trees. It crosses a side stream and returns you to the lower bridge. Keep downhill beside the gorge to retrace your steps back to the car park.

9 Glen Banvie —————————————————————————B

A waymarked circuit on good tracks: up Banvie Burn and back by Bruar Water, with a diversion to see its magnificent waterfalls. Although mainly through forest and mixed woodland, there are also fine views.
Length: **11 miles/17.6km**; *Height Climbed:* **900ft/275m**. O.S. Sheet 43

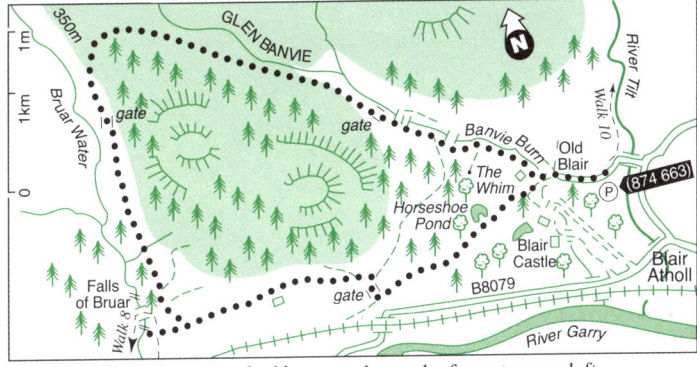

This long circuit is waymarked by occasional orange arrows.

Park in the Glen Tilt car park (*see* Walk 10). Walk out of the car park and turn left along the road. At a crossroads, go left, through Old Blair, then across a bridge over the Banvie Burn. Opposite an archway in the wall on the left, turn right up a track. This runs through trees above the Banvie Burn.

At a sign for 'The Whim' divert left to a folly from which there are fine views. Return to the main track and continue above the burn. Keep left at the next junction (there is a bridge down to your right). At a hairpin bend beyond keep straight on, and when the track forks beyond that, keep left. This leads you through a gate and into the open glen, with trees beyond a fence to your left.

Near the top of the glen the track enters open pine woodland then bends left, down Glen Bruar. Continue down the glen to reach a gate in a deer fence then continue for 1½ miles/2.5km to a T-junction.

Divert to the right for 500m to see the Falls of Bruar (Walk 8), then return to the main track, continuing for 1¼ miles/2km to reach another track junction. Turn right downhill to reach a gate, with a four-way junction just beyond. Turn left on a clear track and follow it into fields.

The track passes Horseshoe Pond then bends right down a Wellingtonia avenue. Take the first left and follow the lane back over the Banvie Burn and through Old Blair. Turn right at the crossroads to return to the start.

10 Glen Tilt   B

A walk up one of Perthshire's finest glens, through pasture and woodland below a grand sweep of mountains. Length: **10 miles/16km** (*Shortcut:* **6 miles/9.6km**); *Height Climbed:* **500ft/150m**.

O.S. Sheet 43

This fine, complex route is marked by occasional yellow arrows.

From the main road through Blair Atholl follow signs for Old Blair and turn left into the Glen Tilt car park (fee). Take the path behind the noticeboard and cross the old packbridge to climb up to a track.

Look for an arrow marking a clear path leaving the main track and heading uphill to the left. The route climbs under tall trees to join a level track. Walk right to the rifle range (a sign indicates an alternative route if the range is in use) and walk below it, going right twice at forks in the track, to reach a junction. For a shortcut head right, crossing Gilbert's Bridge to join the return route. The main route goes left through a gate.

Continuing up the glen, look for a path marked to the right which leads down to a meadow where you join a grassy track through scattered trees above the river. After a bridge over a spectacular gorge there is a viewpoint among ruins 100m above the path.

The path leads to Gow's Bridge. Go right over this and follow a clear track down the far side of the glen.

Watch for an arrow pointing left, by a wooden hut. This leads onto a grassy track, which soon splits. Keep right and continue in order to rejoin the main track.

Later, fork left on another grassy track to climb above farm buildings.

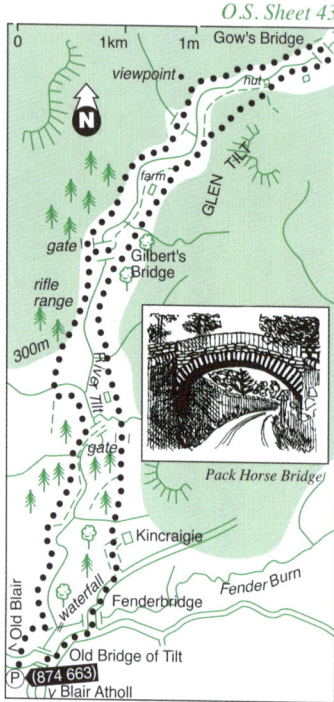

There are fine views from this track. Just beyond a cottage, go through a gate. The arrows peter out from here but the route is in no doubt. Continue straight ahead to reach the entrance road to a house. Go right and follow this to the public road. Go right, downhill, to reach the sign for Old Blair and the car park.

11 Carn Liath   A+

A steep but straightforward ascent of a Munro near Blair Atholl. Clear path and spectacular views. **Length: 6 miles/9.75km** *(there and back);* **Height Climbed: 2220ft/650m.**

O.S. Sheet 43

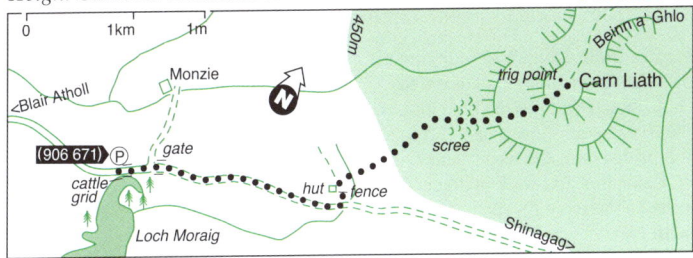

Beinn a' Ghlo, north of Blair Atholl, consists of a number of peaks. Three of these are Munros, the most accessible of which is Carn Liath.

To reach the start, take a minor road north from Blair Atholl signposted to Monzie. Follow this uphill, keeping straight on when a road cuts left for Old Blair. The road climbs steeply to a second signposted junction. Here go right for Monzie and follow the narrow road for 2 miles. There is a car park (fee) to the left of the road, opposite the trees surrounding Loch Moraig.

Start walking along the road, with a good view of the path zig-zagging up the shoulder of Carn Liath ahead. After a short distance turn right, through a gate signposted for 'Shinagag', and follow the clear track beyond for a little over 1 mile/1.6km, until the roof of a hut is visible to the left of the track.

Leave the track here on a grassy path which cuts off to the left. Go through a gate in a fence, pass the hut immediately beyond, and follow the path parallel to a fence to the left for a further 100m, before cutting right on a fainter path along the line of an old dyke. The line of stones briefly disappears in a flat, marshy area, before becoming obvious again on the slope beyond. Follow the dyke until it makes a right-angle turn to the left, then continue straight uphill on a clear path.

Follow this as it climbs over peat then scree to a cairn near the summit, which marks the end of the steepest section of the path. From here the gradient eases for the final walk to the trig point and summit cairn.

The panoramic views are breathtaking. Schiehallion (Walk 7) and Ben Vrackie (Walk 15) to the south, and to the north the higher peaks of Beinn a' Ghlo. The onward path to the next peak (Bràigh Coire Chruinn-bhalgain) is obvious, and may tempt experienced walkers who wish a longer expedition. Return by the same route.

12 **Blair Atholl to Fincastle** B

A linear walk through birchwood, moorland and pasture to pretty Glen Fincastle. Short enough to walk both ways and enjoy the splendid views in either direction. **Length: 3 miles/4.8km** (one way); **Height Climbed: 820ft/250m** (north to south) **425ft/130m** (south to north).

O.S. Sheet 43

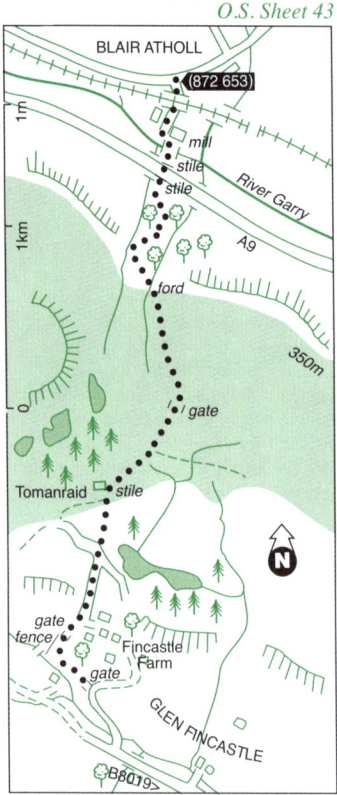

Park in Blair Atholl and walk down past the Watermill, which has a tea shop. Keep on until the road ends at the river then follow a path left to a footbridge over the River Garry.

Cross this and walk up over two stiles to the busy A9 road. **Cross with care** to another stile and climb through trees with a burn to your right; straight at first, and then in a series of zig-zags. The wood narrows and open moorland appears to your left. At this point, the path sets off ahead-left, climbing across the moor towards the watershed.

A wall runs along the watershed. Go through a gate in this, and the rhododendrons beyond, then edge right to follow a grassy path running parallel to a fence. Go through a gate in a fence running across the slope and continue, now with a fence to your left, to reach Tomanraid cottage.

Immediately before the cottage go left over a stile and then go straight downhill on a clear track until it bends left towards farm buildings. At this point keep straight on (Glen Fincastle) on a path between fences.

At the foot of the lane there are two gates. Go through the wooden gate, directly ahead, and continue downhill for a few paces. You quickly join a clearer path which edges left, with an old wall to your left and a slope leading down to a burn to your right. This quickly leads to a gate at the end of the public road.

Return by the same route.

13 Killiecrankie   B

A short, steep, waymarked trail over the wooded crags that overlook the Pass of Killiecrankie. The loop goes through an attractive landscape rich in wildlife. Extensive views. Length: **3 miles/4.8km**; Height Climbed: **820ft/250m**.

O.S. Sheet 43

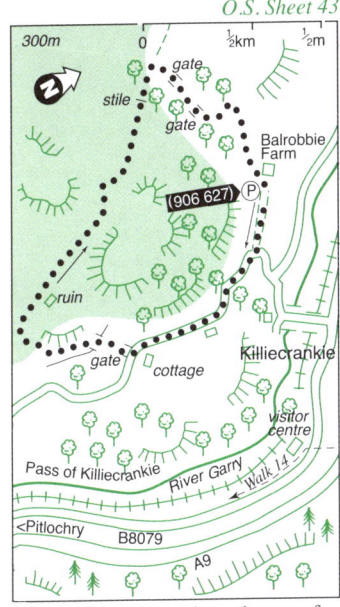

This walk follows a trail, marked with yellow posts, round a former nature reserve.

To reach the walk, take a minor road from the centre of Killiecrankie village, which leads over the railway then the River Garry. After a short distance, follow a second minor road which cuts off to the left and climbs uphill. At a sharp bend, turn right up the access road to Balrobbie Farm. There is a small car park on the left as you approach the farm.

Walk down the driveway and turn right along the road, climbing uphill below the wooded crags. Where the road levels off, opposite a cottage, turn right through a gate. Follow a grassy path to a gate in a stone wall.

Turn left beyond this, climbing diagonally under the crags to reach an iron gate and a bench, beyond which steep zig-zags lead to a delightful area of open marshes and wooded knolls. The grassy path bends right, by a wooded ridge, passing to the left of a ruined cottage. Immediately beyond this the path turns right, onto the ridge, then goes left (arrow).

As you crest the hill there are superb views to Blair Atholl and the mountains beyond. Drop downhill on a clear path and go over a stile back into birch woodland. As you leave the trees there is another bench and the trail turns right, along the top of a field.

After passing through two gates the path edges left to reach a post, then goes straight downhill to reach a second post at the top of some zig-zags down a steep, wooded slope. Below, it heads diagonally right downhill to reach an iron gate. Beyond this the path runs beside a stone wall, passing above Balrobbie Farm, to return to the car park.

Walks Pitlochry & Aberfeldy

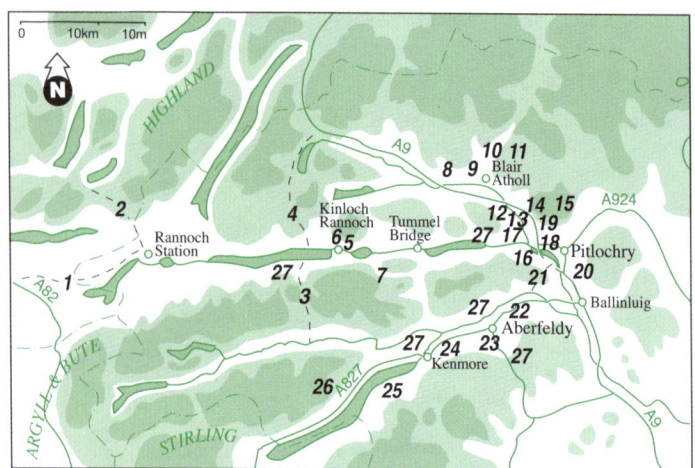

Grades

A+ .... Full walking equipment – including map and compass – and previous hill walking experience essential

A ...... Full walking equipment required

B ...... Strong footwear and waterproof clothing required

C ...... Comfortable footwear recommended

NB: Assume each walk increases at least one grade in winter conditions. Hill routes can become extremely treacherous.

— www.pocketwalks.com —

Published by: *Hallewell Publications, Scotland*
Printed in Scotland

While every care has been taken in the preparation of this guide, the publishers cannot accept responsibility for any loss, damage or injury resulting from its use.

Walks Pitlochry & Aberfeldy

walk		grade
1	Rannoch Moor	A+
2	Corrour to Rannoch Station	A+
3	Carie to Innerwick	A
4	Loch Rannoch to Dalnaspidal	A
5	Kinloch Rannoch	C
6	Craig Varr	B
7	Schiehallion & Foss Loop	A+/C
8	Falls of Bruar	C
9	Glen Banvie	B
10	Glen Tilt	B
11	Carn Liath	A+
12	Blair Atholl to Fincastle	B
13	Killiecrankie	B
14	Moulin to Killiecrankie	B
15	Ben Vrackie	A
16	Loch Faskally	B
17	Linn of Tummel	C
18	Loch Dunmore	C
19	Craigower Hill	B
20	Black Spout	C
21	Pitlochry to Grandtully	B
22	Aberfeldy to Grandtully	C
23	Birks of Aberfeldy	B
24	Kenmore Riverside	C
25	Falls of Acharn	C
26	Ben Lawers & Edramucky Trail	A+/C
27	Forest Walks	B/C

14 Moulin to Killiecrankie _____ B

A circular route using parts of the Pitlochry path network, crossing a moorland pass and returning through woods. Possible links with Walks 15, 16 & 19. Length: **7 miles/11km**; *Height Climbed:* **1500ft/450m**.

O.S. Sheets 43 & 52

To reach the start, follow the instructions for Walk 15. Start as for that route and follow it to the junction marked **X** in the text and on the map.

Head left from the junction (signposted Killiecrankie). Climb steadily, crossing a stile to the left and skirting round the back of a knoll on a now faint path, to reach Bealach na Searmoin. From here a clear track descends, with fine views of the Garry Valley and Blair Castle.

As you descend, a path comes in from the right (signposted Ben Vrackie). Keep straight on (signposted Killiecrankie) and continue on a clear track, crossing a footbridge then a stile by a gate. The grassy track then zig-zags down to a ladder stile. Cross this, head left on a grassy track and follow it to a junction with a tarred road, just to the right of a reservoir. Turn right (signposted Killiecrankie) and follow the road down, under the A9, to join the public road near the village.

Cross the road (carefully) and head left, passing the NTS Visitor Centre (café, shop and toilets). Continue along the pavement for ½ mile/0.8km until you reach a green sign pointing across the road for 'Moulin'. Cross over, go through the gate and walk uphill to the impressive concrete viaduct which carries the A9. Follow the markers, left at first, then climbing by a burn under the A9, then up steps to join a broad forest track.

Turn right and follow this (keeping left at one signposted junction), for 1½ miles/2.5km. A waymarked path (Walk 19) joins from the left. Ignore this. After a few paces a path cuts off the main track to the right (blue marker). Turn onto this and follow it by the golf course, round a garden, then on down a broad track to join the public road. Continue to the fork above Moulin and turn left to return to the car park.

15 Ben Vrackie — A

A varied and scenic climb up the mountain that overlooks Pitlochry. After starting by a wooded stream, the walk crosses heather moorland to a lochan under Ben Vrackie's steep south face. Much work has been done to improve the paths, but the final climb is steep and unrelenting.
Length: **6 miles/9.6km** (there and back); *Height Climbed:* **2150ft/660m**.

O.S. Sheets 43 & 52

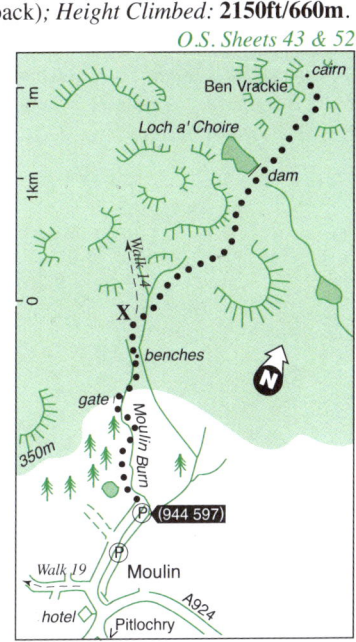

This walk starts from the village of Moulin, a mile to the north of Pitlochry on the A924 Blairgowrie road. Turn left just beyond the Moulin Hotel. At the next junction, go right. Park in one of the two car parks to the right of the road.

Beyond the top car park, follow the 'Bealach Walk', marked with green signs and shown on a map in the car park. Take the path leading out of the car park and up the left side of Moulin Burn. After crossing a track continue up the right side of the burn through mature deciduous woodland. At the next track go left for 100m then follow the path to the right up a smaller stream.

Follow the clear path to a gate at the top of the wood. Beyond this, the path crosses the burn to your right then starts climbing through moorland, passing a pair of benches (where there is a splendid view over Pitlochry) before reaching a clear junction (**X**), where the Bealach Walk climbs uphill to the left (Walk 14). Keep right for Ben Vrackie.

Pass through a gap in the hills, go through a kissing gate and follow the path round craggy slopes to Loch a' Choire. Cross the dam wall to the foot of Ben Vrackie.

Now tackle the hardest part of the walk – the stiff climb on a well-made path up a shallow gully that emerges just to the east of the summit. As the gradient eases bend left to reach the trig point and view indicator cairn. Take time to survey the many distant landmarks before returning by the outward route.

16 Loch Faskally / 17 Linn of Tummel / 18 Loch Dunmore ———————— B/C/C

16) *A long, low-level circuit of a scenic loch, using woodland paths and a quiet minor road. With several car parks en route, you can do the walk in short sections. Length: up to* **8 miles/12.8km**; *Height Climbed: negligible.* **17)** *A marked nature trail past rapids on the River Tummel. Length:* **2 miles/3.2km**; *Height Climbed:* **250ft/75m**. **18)** *Two easy woodland trails round Loch Dunmore, or a little further round Dunmore Hill. Length:* **¾-1½ miles/1.2-2km**; *Height Climbed: negligible. Possible extension from 16 or 17 to visitor centre at Killiecrankie.*

O.S. Sheets 43 & 52

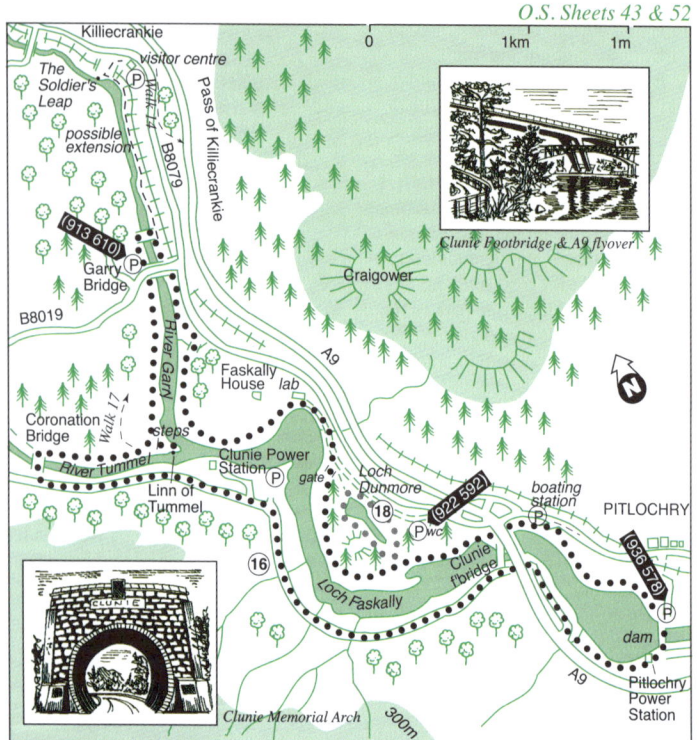

Loch Faskally was created in 1950 as part of a hydro-electric scheme. Pitlochry Dam holds back the water that supplies Pitlochry Power Station. It is famous for its fish ladder where you can see salmon passing upstream, by-passing the dam. The loch has wooded shores that provide very pleasant walking. At its head the rivers Garry and Tummel meet; the latter tumbling over rocky rapids.

Walk 16) From the centre of Pitlochry follow signs to Pitlochry Dam. There is a car park just before you cross the top of the dam wall. On the far side turn right, following a green sign for the 'Killiecrankie Path'. You quickly reach a fork. Keep right here and continue to join the minor road to Clunie. Go right along this, under the A9 flyover and past the Clunie footbridge (a short cut back to Pitlochry).

Stroll along the quiet road for 2 miles/3km. At Clunie Power Station it is worth looking at the plaques on the memorial arch. There is a car park and picnic site on the shore here.

After Clunie the road bends left up the River Tummel. Look for a signposted path to the right (Garry Bridge). This leads to the Coronation Bridge – a handsome suspension bridge. Cross this and turn right down the far bank of the river. In $^1\!/_2$ mile/0.8km, when the path bends left, detour down steps to the bank and upstream a little to see the Linn of Tummel.

Continue on the main path, now following the River Garry. After passing under a high road bridge the path climbs to a junction. (Heading left takes you to a car park beside the bridge). Turn right for a short distance and cross a footbridge with excellent views of the gorge.

Now there is a choice. If you turn to the left a walk of 1 mile/1.6km (2 miles/3km there and back) leads through the narrow, wooded Pass of Killiecrankie to a National Trust for Scotland information centre. The centre provides information on the Battle of Killiecrankie (1689), fought nearby between a Jacobite army under Graham of Claverhouse ('Bonnie Dundee') and the supporters of William III. Claverhouse was victorious, but died after the battle. The athletic escape of one of the defeated army is remembered at 'The Soldier's Leap': a narrow part of the river across which he is said to have jumped.

To continue on the main route, turn right on a path that soon goes back under the road bridge. You are now on the 'Bealach Walk', which is marked with green signs. The

Pitlochry Dam

path kinks left beside a side stream and crosses it by a footbridge then goes right again, back to the river. Now there are fields on the left, and Loch Faskally starts to the right.

After passing the Freshwater Fisheries Laboratory walk along the tarmac drive beside the loch. Once back into woods, look for a vehicle track to the right signposted for Pitlochry. Follow this past a gate and on through Faskally Wood (white markers). The wood has a car park and more marked trails (*see* Walk 18).

The track loops through the wood, eventually becoming a path, then leads down wooden steps to the loch shore. Stay on the lochside path, walking by the end of Clunie Footbridge and under the A9 flyover. Soon the path bends left to the Boating Station, where there is a café.

Follow the public road beyond back towards Pitlochry. Just before you reach the main road, Lagreach Brae cuts right and you have a choice. To reach the town centre, continue to the road and turn right. To return to the dam, turn right, through houses, to join a signposted path by the loch.

Walk 17) This walk follows a National Trust for Scotland nature trail. To start at the Garry Bridge car park on the B8019, drive north out of Pitlochry and turn left at the sign for Kinloch Rannoch. Park at the far end of the bridge.

Go down steps by a display board beside the bridge. Walk down a tarred track and turn right on the path under the road bridge (signposted

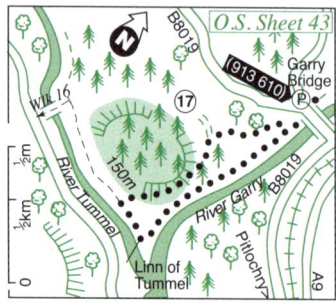

for Linn of Tummel). A few yellow arrows mark the trail.

Follow the path all the way down the River Garry until it bends right up the River Tummel. Here detour down steps to a monolith marking Queen Victoria's visit then walk upstream for a closer view of the Linn, which was a waterfall before the waters of Loch Faskally were raised.

Back on the main path, continue upstream for 300m then go uphill on a path to the right. Turn right on the track above and follow it back round the hill. At the edge of the trees take a path to the right between fences and follow it round the edge of a field to rejoin the outward path just before the road bridge.

Walk 18) An easy stroll through mixed woodland on the edge of Loch Faskally. Head north from Pitlochry and turn left into the car park just beyond the A9 road junction.

The short walk, marked with red posts, circuits secluded Loch Dunmore, with its picturesque bridge. The longer white trail loops round Dunmore Hill on good, level tracks.

19 Craigower Hill   B

This hill behind Pitlochry gives wonderful views. A fairly short trail, steep in places, leads across a golf course and through conifers to the open summit, then loops back down a forest road. Length: **3½ miles/5.6km**; *Height Climbed:* **725ft/220m**.

O.S. Sheets 43 & 52

Craigower ('goat's crag') is a rocky promontory high above the A9. The summit is cared for by the National Trust for Scotland.

At the north end of Pitlochry drive (or walk) up Larchwood Road, past a pond and the golf club, to a T-junction. Go left here and park in the Craigower car park.

Walk on up the road, which turns into a track. Enter the golf course and take the right fork towards a red-roofed cottage. The track crosses the fairways, so watch out for golfers.

Just before the cottage gate, head left on a path which goes round the cottage then runs left along the edge of the wood. There are super views back down to Pitlochry from a carved bench. Follow the path on through the trees up to a forest track.

Walk left on the track for a few metres then turn right on a small path. The path climbs on a carpet of larch needles, becoming steeper towards the top. Where it exits the plantation it bends right to go diagonally up the slope through scattered trees. The path bends left after a short distance, climbing to the viewpoint indicator.

Go left to a bench overlooking Loch Faskally to the south, then return to look west up Loch Tummel towards Glencoe. The conical peak on the left is Schiehallion (Walk 7).

Take the small path dropping downhill ahead. Go right at a post, with trees to your right, to reach a forest track. Go right along this, downhill, and after two zig-zags to the right look for a path to the left This is the way you came up. Turn down the path and retrace the route back across the golf course.

20 Black Spout _____C

A short circuit from Pitlochry through oak woodland to a fine waterfall. The full walk continues across fields to one of Scotland's smallest distilleries – omitting it shortens the route by 1 mile/1.6km. A similar distance is saved by starting from the car park. Length: **1-3 miles/1.6-4.8km**; Height Climbed: **250-350ft/75-100m**. *O.S. Sheet 52 or 53*

Walk down Pitlochry's main street in the direction of Perth, under the railway bridge and past the distillery. Turn left up a well-signed track to the Black Spout car park, which is an alternative start point. This route follows the 'Edradour Path', which is way-marked by yellow signs.

Keep going up the track, round a double bend and past the pitch and putt course. At a signposted junction go right (Black Spout). Keep left at a bench to reach a further junction and go right (Black Spout). This leads to the viewpoint for the Black Spout waterfall.

Continue uphill. The path pulls away from the burn and reaches a junction. Go right (Edradour). At a fork just beyond, go right. This quickly leads to a four-way junction by the corner of a field. Go straight on (Edradour), up the field edge.

The path joins the public road opposite the Edradour Distillery. Walk left along the road and turn left when you see a sign for a path to Pitlochry. This path runs between the road and a field for a short distance, then turns left down the field edge. When the houses to your right end there is a further junction. Go left and follow a path to reenter the oak wood.

Keep straight on at two junctions, then go right at a fork (off the main track). Descend until you reach a T-junction. **To reach the Black Spout car park** go left and immediately left again. **To return to Pitlochry**, turn right and descend to the Kinnaird Burn. Cross a bridge and go left. Keep right at the next junction, then keep left when the path reaches a tarred access road. Follow this to the main road and turn right to return to the town centre.

21 **Pitlochry to Grandtully** ───────────── B

A linear walk over a wooded ridge, passing a small stone circle.
Delightful views of Strath Tay. Length: **4½ miles/7.2km** (one way);
Height Climbed: **900ft/275m**. *Possible link with Walk 22.*   O.S. Sheet 52

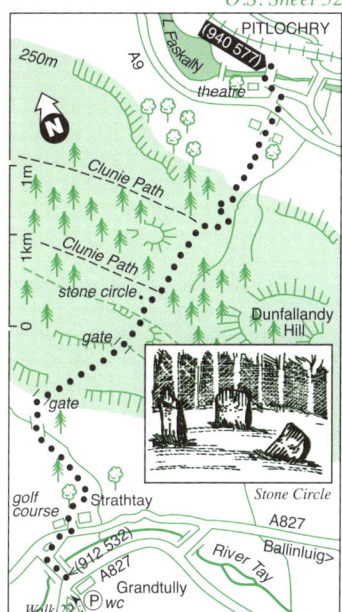

Stone Circle

This walk can be done in either direction, but the views are better walking south as described.

From the middle of Pitlochry follow signs for the Theatre. These lead to a footbridge. Cross this and turn left up to a road junction. Head straight over and up a drive, signed 'Strathtay'. This leads to the A9.

Go straight over (**take great care**) and up a road through farm buildings. A track continues uphill into the forest, then zig-zags. Watch for a signposted path heading off to the left (Strathtay) and follow it through a gate. (**NB:** If you go straight on here, you are on the 'Clunie Path' – a circuit leading to a good viewpoint. Navigation is tricky at the far end, so take an OS map if you want to try it.)

The rough path climbs to join a forest track – edge left to join a signposted path which initially runs parallel to the track then pulls away. Follow this to a junction with forest tracks (the 'Clunie Path' rejoins here from your right). Walk straight on along a track. In 200m a rough path heads right to reach a stone circle.

Return to the track and continue. Keep straight on at a four-way junction, visible ahead. Shortly beyond this the track turns hard left. At this point keep straight on, passing through a metal gate.

The path now runs down and across the grassy slope before entering trees by a burn. Run by this for a short way, then cross it on a bridge and continue down the far side.

Beyond this the path is clear; by the burn at first, then pulling away to reach the golf course. Cross a narrow part of the course (with care) then turn down an access road to reach the public road.

Turn right, then keep left to cross the bridge over the river to Grandtully.

22 Aberfeldy to Grandtully _____ C

A low-level, lineal walk through farmland and woodland by the River Tay. Possible link with Walk 21. Length: **4 miles/6.5km** (one way); Height Climbed: negligible.

O.S. Sheet 52

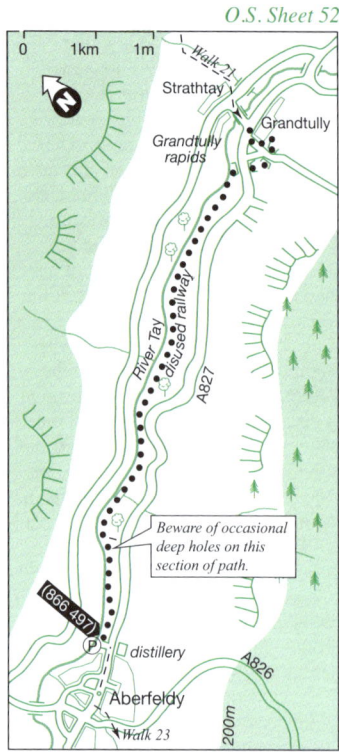

From the centre of Aberfeldy, drive eastward by the A827, signposted for Pitlochry and the A9. (If you walk from the centre, it adds around ½ mile/0.8km to the walk). On the edge of the village you pass the distillery to your right, then the cemetery to your left. Turn left immediately beyond the cemetery to find a rough parking area to the left.

A signpost marks the start of the walk, which begins as a path by the road before dropping down to your left to run through the trees beside the River Tay. After ½ mile/0.8km you reach a signposted junction. Keep left here (Grandtully). The river now bends away from the road, and you walk along the edge of a narrow band of trees with a field to your right, crossing a footbridge along the way.

Half way to Grandtully (pronounced 'Grantly'), the path edges right, climbing gently to join the old railway line (a spur line from Ballinluig to Aberfeldy, closed in 1965; now part of the Rob Roy Way). Follow this clear straight path.

As you approach Grandtully, the track passes under two stone road bridges. Just beyond the second bridge, go left (Rob Roy Way), passing through a car park to join a public road. Go right and follow the road down to the main road through the village.

The village is small, but there is an inn and a chocolate shop/café, and a short detour down the Strathtay road leads to a view of the rapids (much used by canoeists) and a possible link with Walk 21.

Return by the same route.

23 Birks of Aberfeldy — B

A steep circuit round the Falls of Moness, one of the finest waterfalls in Perthshire. The walk passes the spot where Robert Burns composed a song about the wooded glen and its roaring falls. Length: **2½ miles/4km**; *Height Climbed:* **550ft/170m**.

O.S. Sheet 52

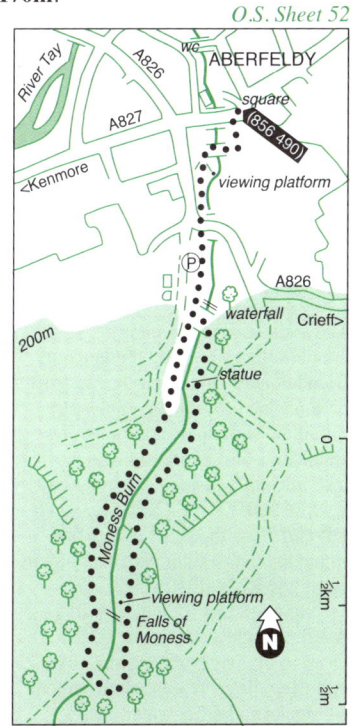

The Scots word 'Birks' means birch trees: just one of the tree and plant species that grow prolifically in this moist, sheltered glen.

Start in the centre of the attractive market town of Aberfeldy. From the Square, walk in the direction of Kenmore to the bridge over the Moness Burn. Just before the bridge, turn left, passing under the stone arch of the war memorial, and follow the path across the burn and walk upstream to the A826 Crieff road.

Cross the road and continue uphill through lower and upper car parks. Soon the path divides – take the left fork over a footbridge above a small waterfall.

The path climbs steeply, using footbridges to cross the tumbling side streams. You ascend past a series of falls and a rock ledge where Burns was inspired by the view. Wooden steps, walkways and railings ease the climb and give safe views of the best features. Where the path steepens in zig-zags there is a viewing platform for the main Falls of Moness, a spectacular drop of 80ft (25m).

Continue uphill to a bridge that spans the top of the Falls where they plunge over a rock sill. Cross over to the other side. When you reach a junction, turn right, and follow the path as it bends back downhill through the woods. There are fewer views on this side, but the vegetation is just as rich.

Follow the path down to the car parks and cross them and the road to return by your outward path to the centre of Aberfeldy.

24 Kenmore Riverside — C

A riverside walk from the shore of Loch Tay downstream by the River Tay, returning through the pretty village of Kenmore. **Length: 3 miles/ 4.8km**; *Height Climbed:* negligible.

O.S. Sheet 51 or 52

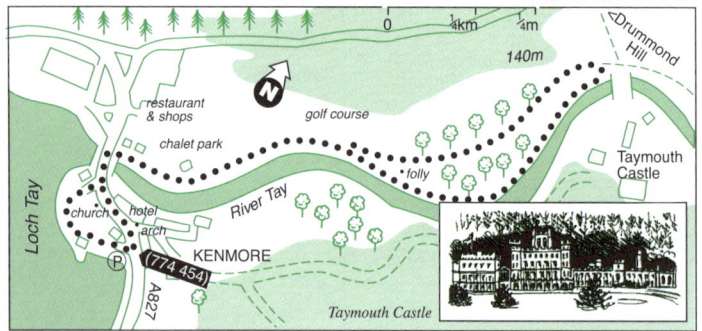

The walk begins in Kenmore, a 'model village' built by the lairds of Breadalbane. Start from the car park on the edge of Loch Tay and walk round the shore past pontoons. The small lane runs along the wooded lochside and joins the main road by a white house – the 'Orphanage'. Go left and cross the stone bridge and immediately go right on to a footpath along the River Tay.

Although this is an easy walk, watch that children do not go too close to the river, which runs swift and deep. It is an ideal environment for ducks and other water birds, which can be spotted on the water.

Follow the clear path past a chalet park on the left. When you reach a fork just beyond the end of the park go right, leaving the main path and following a clear, narrow path which drops towards the river bank. Follow this by the river until a bridge becomes visible ahead, then go left to join a clear track.

A turn to the right at this point leads to a link with the Drummond Hill forest walks (*see* Walk 27), but for this walk go left and follow the track for just over a mile/1.6km to reach an old folly – a tower with a spiral staircase. (NB: take care on the stairs if you go inside.)

Just beyond, you rejoin the original path. Retrace your steps to Kenmore and cross back over the old bridge. This time keep on the main road. Walk past the church into the centre of the village, past white timbered cottages built by the 3rd Earl in 1760 and the even older Kenmore Hotel, which dates from 1572. The road bends right, past an archway with elaborate gates, to take you back to the car park.

25 Falls of Acharn _____ C

A short but vigorous circular walk round a dramatic wooded gorge above Loch Tay. At the Hermit's Cave a tunnel leads to a breathtaking view of the high waterfall, whilst further up smaller cascades flow through the smoothly carved rock. Length: **1½ miles/2km**; *Height Climbed:* **400ft/120m**.

O.S. Sheet 51 or 52

The walk starts from the South Loch Tay road, 2 miles outside Kenmore in the hamlet of Acharn. There is limited parking just beyond the stone bridge at the start of the walk.

Follow the sign for the Falls up the hard stony track on the left. After the houses there is a steady haul upwards. Just after the track bends right there is a sign on the left for 'Hermit's Cave'. Walk into the dark cave entrance, allowing time for your eyes to adjust before continuing through the tunnel. Half way along turn left, down shallow steps to a platform for a terrific view of the precipitous fall.

Return through the tunnel, this time going left to leave the cave by the top exit. Continue up the track, climbing steadily until it bends left. On the next corner take the path signposted left to the 'Viewing Platform'. Here a wooden walkway crosses the burn giving close views of it tumbling over sculpted rock.

You can return down the far bank from this point, or go back to the track and continue another 100m to the 'Upper Bridge'. Cross the burn by the bridge and immediately turn left through a kissing gate. Walk under spreading beeches down the far side, looking right to see Loch Tay.

Follow the path all the way back down this side, with glimpses of falls on the left. As you drop look for occasional views across to the Hermit's Cave. Continue down the path to Acharn and at the road go left over the bridge back to the starting point.

26 Ben Lawers & Edramucky Trail _____ A+/C

A) *A steep hill climb on rocky paths up Perthshire's highest mountain. Beinn Ghlas (also a Munro) is climbed on the way. Length:* **6½ miles/ 10.4km** *(there and back); Height Climbed:* **3080ft/940m**. **B)** *A short circuit on the lower slopes of Ben Lawers. Length:* up to **1½ miles/3km**; *Height Climbed:* up to **655ft/200m**.

O.S. Sheet 51

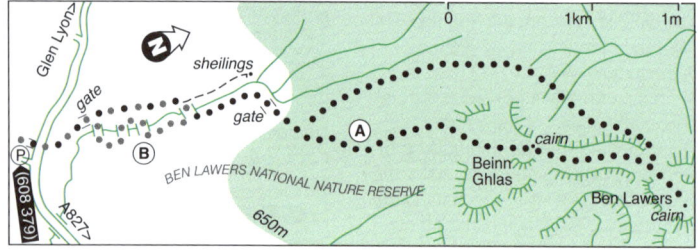

The area around Ben Lawers is a National Nature Reserve. To reach the car park, look for the minor road signposted to Ben Lawers heading north from the A827, 12 miles west of Kenmore and 4½ miles east of Killin.

Follow this for 2½ miles to reach the car park (fee) to the left of the road. The walks start from an interpretive board, just inside the car park on the right. Follow the waymarked path from here through a wooden gate. Cross the public road and continue on the clear path until it splits.

A) To climb Ben Lawers, keep left and follow the signposted path. This climbs, crosses the burn and continues upward on the far side with a fence off to the right.

The path passes through two gates then climbs steeply up the shoulder of Beinn Ghlas. The summit is marked by a small cairn – be careful of cliffs on the north side. The views are excellent, including a profile of Ben Lawers directly ahead.

Continue over the top and down to the col between Beinn Ghlas and Ben Lawers, then on up to the second summit, over the rockiest ground of the day. From the cairn on top of Ben Lawers you can see for miles.

Return to the col between the mountains and fork right at the low point to return on a path skirting the back of Beinn Ghlas. At the next col the path crosses a line of old fence posts and continues down the left side of the valley. It rejoins the outward path just before the fenced enclosure. Turn right, go through the two gates, then retrace your steps to the car park.

B) To follow the Edramucky Trail, go right, and follow the waymarked circuit as it climbs, crossing and re-crossing the burn.

A leaflet available in the car park gives details of the points of interest along the way.

27 Forest Walks — B/C

All but one of these walks lie within Tay Forest Park, which consists of many separate forests covering some of the finest landscapes in Highland Perthshire. The following entries highlight waymarked walks varying in length from just under ½ mile/0.8km to 5¾ miles/9.2km. The colour coded trails pass through a variety of woodland habitats, visiting viewpoints and other features of interest within the forests.

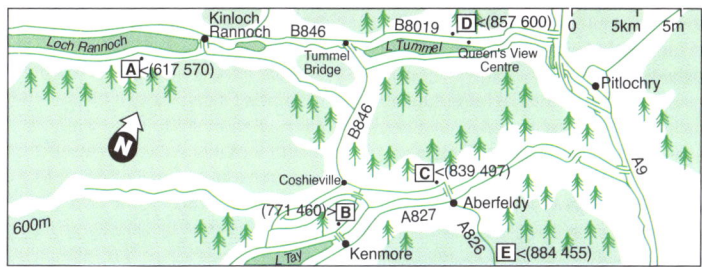

Tay Forest Park is managed by Forestry & Land Scotland, the body responsible for all Scotland's publicly owned forests. They encourage access with the provision of car parks, picnic areas, map boards and signed paths. A leaflet about the park is available at the Queen's View Visitor Centre on the edge of Loch Tummel or online.

Within the woods you could get a glimpse of red squirrels, roe deer and many woodland birds, including the turkey-like capercaillie. As well as being important for wildlife and recreation, the forests are used to produce timber, so there may be thinning and felling operations in progress and occasionally a walk may be closed or diverted for public safety.

A: Rannoch Forest (Grade C)
Carie Walk *(red)* ½ mile/0.8km;
Kilvrecht Walk *(blue)* 1½ miles/2km; **Allt Na Bogair Walk** *(yellow)* 5½ miles/8km. (*See* also Walk 3).

Start in the Carie car park, 3 miles/5km along the south Loch Rannoch road from Kinloch Rannoch.

The two shorter walks meander through deciduous woodland beside the river and campsite. The longer one climbs upstream through conifer woodland before returning down a clear forest track

Rannoch Forest

and a path passing a fine viewpoint. Near the top of the walk you will pass examples of old Scots pine trees. These give a flavour of the nearby Black Wood of Rannoch, a remnant of ancient Caledonian forest.

B: Drummond Hill (Grade C)
Black Rock Walk *(blue)* $2^{3}/_{4}$ miles/4.4km; **Taymouth Walk** *(red)* $2^{1}/_{2}$ miles/4km; **Caisteal MacTuathal** *(marked by standing stones)* $5^{3}/_{4}$ miles/9.2km.

Drummond Hill is a long, forested ridge overlooking Kenmore and Loch Tay. It is where capercaillie were reintroduced in 1837 after they had become extinct in Scotland. From Kenmore, cross the bridge over the River Tay and turn right on the minor road to Tummel Bridge. After 400m the car park is up a track on the left.

All routes start up the same forest track. The red and blue routes do roughly the same amount of climbing; blue heads west to Black Rock for a view over Kenmore, while the red route contours east. The longer route climbs to the site of an old fort with fine views over Loch Tay and Glen Lyon.

C: Weem (Grade C)
Weem Walk *(red)* 1mile/1.6km.

Weem Wood is on the opposite side of the Tay valley from Aberfeldy. It is a steep craggy hillside covered in mainly deciduous trees. Leave Aberfeldy by crossing the Wade Bridge and turn right after the Weem Hotel where the forest walk is signed.

The walk zig-zags uphill to St David's Well, a hermit's retreat under an overhanging cliff. At various points along the route there are fine views through the trees to Aberfeldy. It is quite rocky underfoot with many steps along the way.

D: Allean (Grade C)
Clachan Trail *(yellow)* $1^{3}/_{4}$ miles/3km; **Ring Fort Trail** *(red)* $2^{1}/_{2}$ miles/4km.

Allean is the forested area on the north side of Loch Tummel. The walks car park is off the B8019, just west of the Queen's View Visitor Centre. Before starting the walks, it is worth looking at the view itself: a famous view up Loch Tummel to Schiehallion, which is one of the most popular images of the area.

The two walks both start with a steady climb up a forest track to visit a viewpoint and a ruined 18th-century settlement. The longer walk also passes an 8th-century ring fort.

E: Griffin Forest (Grade B)
Loch Kennard $4^{1}/_{2}$ miles/7km.

Griffin Forest is a large private forest (ie, **not** part of Tay Forest Park) between Aberfeldy and Dunkeld. To reach the car park, drive 4 miles south from Aberfeldy on the A826.

There are a number of well-signposted tracks through the mostly conifer forest. The easiest walk is a pleasant circular route around Loch Kennard. After the initial spur from the car park, this can be done in either direction.

Junctions are well signposted, but you would be advised to photograph the map in the car park to help with navigation.